America's HIDDEN Animal Treasures

Ringtail

Miner's Cat

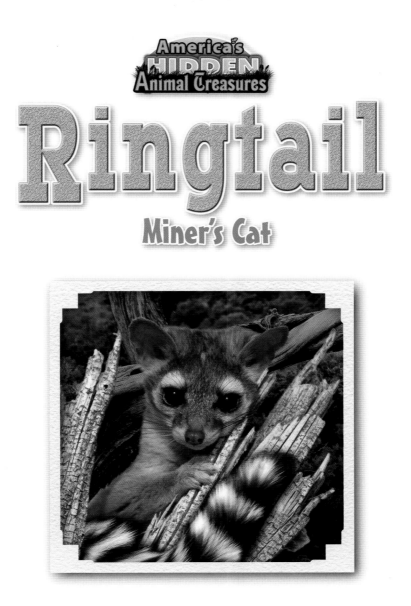

by Joyce Markovics

Consultant: Shane J. Kiefer, CWB®
Plateau Land & Wildlife Management

BEARPORT
PUBLISHING

New York, New York

Credits

Cover and Title Page, © Daniel J. Cox/Natural Exposures; 4, © Jutta C. Burger/Irvine Ranch Conservancy; 5, © Jutta C. Burger/Irvine Ranch Conservancy; 6, © Animals Animals/SuperStock; 7L, © Gerard Lacz/age fotostock/SuperStock; 7R, © Marty Cordano; 8T, © Kenneth W. Fink/Ardea; 8B, © Jarenwicklund/depositphotos/Pixmac; 9, © Phil A. Dotson/Photo Researchers/Getty Images; 10, © Dave Welling; 11L, © Dave Welling; 11R, © Nathan W. Feldman; 12, © Nomad/SuperStock; 13, © Kitchin & Hurst/Leesonphoto; 14, © Minden Pictures/SuperStock; 15L, © Marty Cordano; 15R, © Nathan W. Feldman; 16, © Douglas J. Long; 17T, © Jack Wilburn/Animals Animals-Earth Scenes; 17B, © Terrence McCarthy; 18, © NHPA/SuperStock; 19, © Animals Animals/SuperStock; 20, © Animals Animals/SuperStock; 21, © Animals Animals/SuperStock; 22, © Animals Animals/SuperStock; 23, © Animals Animals/SuperStock; 24T, © Jim Parkin/Shutterstock; 24B, © zhaoliang70/Shutterstock; 25, © Angela Lau; 26, © David Wyatt; 27, © Daniel J. Cox/Natural Exposures; 28, © Tatiana Gettelman; 29, © Jack Wilburn/Animals Animals-Earth Scenes.

Publisher: Kenn Goin
Senior Editor: Lisa Wiseman
Creative Director: Spencer Brinker
Design: Dawn Beard Creative
Photo Researcher: We Research Pictures

Library of Congress Cataloging-in-Publication Data

Markovics, Joyce L.
  Ringtail : miner's cat / by Joyce Markovics.
    p. cm. — (America's hidden animal treasures)
  Includes bibliographical references and index.
  ISBN 978-1-61772-580-7 (library binding) — ISBN 1-61772-580-3 (library binding)
  1. Cacomistle—Juvenile literature. 2. Cacomistle—Behavior—Juvenile literature. I. Title.
  QL737.C26M37 2013
  599.76'3—dc23

                          2012007085

For more information, write to Bearport Publishing Company, Inc., 45 West 21st Street, Suite 3B, New York, New York 10010. Printed in the United States of America in North Mankato, Minnesota.

10 9 8 7 6 5 4 3 2 1

Contents

A Surprise Guest 4

Where's Home? 6

Big Eyes, Bigger Appetite 8

Feeding at Night 10

Expert Hunters 12

Fast Attack! 14

Up Close with Ringtails 16

Starting a Family 18

Growing Up 20

How Many Ringtails? 22

Shrinking Habitat 24

The Future 26

Ringtail Facts 28

People Helping Ringtails 29

Glossary 30

Bibliography 31

Read More 31

Learn More Online 31

Index 32

About the Author 32

A Surprise Guest

It was just before lunchtime on May 23, 2011. The employees at an office building in Irvine, California, had just discovered a strange, furry visitor feasting on a bucket of fried chicken in their conference room. The animal was small and raccoon-like, with huge eyes and a long, puffy ringed tail. The employees had never seen anything like it. What could it be? They phoned the experts at Irvine **Animal Control**, who rushed to the building to help.

No one knows how the animal (shown here) got into the building. It might have entered the conference room after it smelled the fried chicken.

The animal control experts quickly identified the animal. It was a ringtail! They caught the young male with a net and guided him into a special carrying case. Later that day, they brought the ringtail to a nearby **preserve**. There, with **ecologist** Jutta Burger's help, they safely released him back into the wild. Jutta watched as the animal dashed out of the case and disappeared into a hole in a tree. "I must say it seemed to really like its new home," said Jutta.

The captured ringtail (shown here) was released into a wooded area known as the Irvine Ranch Natural Landmarks, where it quickly found a new home.

Although they are sometimes called ringtail cats, ringtails are not actually cats. In fact, they are closely related to raccoons and **coatis**.

Where's Home?

Although ringtails live throughout the Midwest, the western United States, and Mexico, they are rarely ever seen. One reason is that they are active at night, when people are asleep. Another reason is that they are mostly **solitary** animals that tend to avoid people. Lastly, the colors of their coats help them blend into their environment so well that they are difficult to spot. While these reasons make ringtails hard to study, they haven't stopped **biology** professor David Wyatt.

Ringtails in the Wild

CANADA

ME
WA
MT   ND   MN   VT NH MA
OR   NY   RI
ID   WY   SD   WI   MI   PA   CT
NE   IA   OH   NJ
NV   UT   UNITED STATES   IL   IN   WV   DE
CA   CO   KS   MO   KY   VA   MD
AZ   NM   OK   AR   TN   NC
MS   AL   GA   SC   Atlantic
TX   LA   Ocean

Pacific
Ocean

FL

MEXICO

N
W   E
S

☐ Where ringtails live

The color of this ringtail's coat allows it to blend in easily with the colors of its desert home.

David has spent more than 20 years tracking and studying these curious little animals. According to David, ringtails make their homes in forests, deserts, canyons, and rocky **plateaus**. They often choose places near rivers so that they can easily get a drink of fresh water. Basically, David said, "ringtails thrive anywhere they can find food."

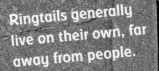

Ringtails generally live on their own, far away from people.

A ringtail in its den

During the day, ringtails sleep in hollow trees and rock **crevices**. These sleeping places are called **dens**. Ringtails sometimes line them with dried grasses so that they are more comfortable.

Big Eyes, Bigger Appetite

Ringtails are small animals. Including their 12- to 17-inch (30- to 43-cm) bushy tails, they measure 24 to 32 inches (61 to 81 cm) long and weigh less than a typical house cat. Despite their small size, ringtails have a pretty big appetite. They will devour just about anything they can find!

A ringtail (top) weighs only up to three pounds (1.4 kg). A typical house cat (bottom) can weigh as much as 8 pounds (3.6 kg).

The ringtail's diet includes small **mammals**, such as mice, as well as fruit, nuts, leaves, and bird and **reptile** eggs. They also have been known to feast on other small animals, such as birds, snakes, and lizards, as well as on dead animals they find. However, insects and spiders, when available, make up a large part of their diet. What's their favorite summertime dinner? They like to eat grasshoppers, crickets, beetles, and spiders—and lots of them!

Ringtails have a fox-like face and a raccoon-like tail. The name *ringtail* comes from the black and white rings found on the animal's tail.

There are between 14 and 16 bands on a ringtail's tail.

Feeding at Night

Ringtails look for insects and other tasty snacks at night. These amazing animals have **adapted** to looking for food in the dark in many ways. For example, their large, round eyes allow them to see in the moonlight. Ringtails also have a superb sense of smell. They can pick up the scent of their **prey** from far away—even when they can't see it in the darkness. Ringtails' ears help them find food, too. They are large and set far apart, allowing ringtails to detect the sounds of tiny animals rustling in the distance.

Ringtails have a special lining on the backs of their huge eyes. This lining reflects light and helps them see better at night.

Ringtails have to be careful when they're out at night looking for food. Great horned owls, which are also **nocturnal**, often hunt them.

In addition, ringtails have special whiskers called **vibrissae** that also help them search for food. Most mammals have whiskers near their mouths. Ringtails, however, also have whiskers around their eyes and on their wrists to help them find their prey when it is too dark to see.

Long whiskers help ringtails search for food and also detect danger.

This ringtail is using its nose to help it find food.

Expert Hunters

Being nocturnal has not stopped ringtails from becoming expert hunters. In spite of their short legs, they are very **agile**, climbing and jumping with the grace of an acrobat. They use the sharp claws on their front and back paws to grip rocks and trees as they move quickly through their **habitat**.

Ringtails are able to quickly climb up and down trees.

Ringtails have five toes on each foot. Each toe has a sharp, curved claw.

What else makes ringtails such great hunters? It's their shape. They have long, narrow bodies that allow them to squeeze into tight spaces to chase after prey. They also use their tails, which are as long as their bodies, to keep their balance. This helps them dart up and down uneven surfaces, such as cliffs, trees, or even cacti, to grab a meal.

A ringtail is able to easily squeeze its thin body between rocks.

Fast Attack!

As ringtails travel over steep cliffs chasing prey, their amazingly **flexible** back feet help them. A human foot can **rotate** only 90 degrees. Ringtails, however, can rotate their back feet 180 degrees. As a result, ringtails' back feet can turn forward, sideways, and all the way backward! This ability helps the animal move rapidly down a steep tree or ledge without falling.

Ringtails are extremely quiet when they are looking for food. This helps them sneak up on their prey and avoid predators.

Ringtails move quickly when they are chasing down prey. Once they are within reach of their target, ringtails pounce. They grab their prey with their sharp teeth and claws. Then it's time to eat. Though ringtails are fierce hunters, "they're right up there with sea otters on the cuteness scale," said David Wyatt.

A ringtail's teeth may be small, but they are very sharp.

Ringtails are sometimes called miner's cats. The name was first used in the mid- to late 1800s, when miners in California and Arizona kept ringtails as pets. The miners admired the ringtails for their mouse-hunting skills.

Up Close with Ringtails

To learn even more about ringtails, David studies them closely in an area of California called Sutter Buttes. In April 2010, he and several students set traps to safely catch and **tag** ringtails living in the wild. Using a mixture of raspberry jelly and cat food, they were able to lure two ringtails into wire cages.

David holding one of the ringtails he caught in Sutter Buttes

Sutter Buttes is a small mountain range located in the north-central part of California.

After shutting the cage doors with the ringtails inside, David and his team examined the animals to make sure they were healthy. Then he placed **radio collars** on them. The collars track the ringtails' movements when the animals are released back into the wild. David can then find out more about where and how they live.

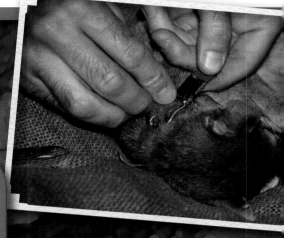

A radio collar being put on a ringtail

One of the captured ringtails was nicknamed "Pigpen" by David and his students. Why? Before it was trapped in the cage, it rolled in the jelly and cat food mixture and then in a pile of dirt! Before releasing him, David and his team gave Pigpen a quick bath.

Pigpen being released after his bath

Starting a Family

Through his research, David has learned that each adult ringtail has its own **territory**—an area where it makes its home and finds food. A ringtail's territory can typically range anywhere from 50 to 100 acres (20 to 40 hectares), though it can vary depending on the ringtail's habitat. During the **mating season**, which happens in late winter or early spring, males and females mark their territory with urine and droppings. They do this to attract a mate.

Ringtails live alone, except during the mating season, when male and female ringtails live together.

About 50 days after mating, a female ringtail gives birth to a **litter** of babies in a den. At birth, baby ringtails are completely helpless. They are unable to see or hear, and they have almost no fur and no rings on their tails. They get all the food they need by drinking milk from their mother's body. Both parents care for their babies until they are old enough to be on their own.

Baby ringtails usually have all their fur by five to six weeks of age.

When they are born, baby ringtails weigh less than one ounce (28 grams)—that's about the weight of a strawberry! There are usually two to four babies in each litter.

Growing Up

Baby ringtails grow quickly. After about two months, they stop drinking milk from their mother and begin to eat the same food as their parents. Then, after about four months, they begin to look like small adults. Their fur becomes darker in color, and white and black bands develop on their tails.

Ringtail babies are very playful. Playing helps them learn how to hunt and care for themselves.

To communicate with each other, young ringtails and their parents make many different sounds, such as barks, chirps, growls, and howls. Scientists are not sure what they all mean, but they know that they play an important role in how ringtails talk to one another.

Baby ringtails make special sounds to communicate with their mothers, especially when they are upset.

Once young ringtails become adults, around two years of age, they are ready to start their own families.

How Many Ringtails?

How many ringtails live in the wild? The question is not easy to answer. Ringtails are small and blend in with their environment. As a result, they are extremely hard to count. David says that even when he's picking up radio signals and knows from a ringtail's collar that the animal is right in front of him, he often still can't see it!

What scientists do know is that ringtails are numerous in some states, including parts of California. However, in other areas of California, where many ringtails once lived, they are now far less common—or worse, almost **extinct**.

Many ringtails live in the deserts of Arizona.

The people of Arizona like the ringtail so much that they made it the state mammal on August 13, 1986.

Shrinking Habitat

Why are ringtails becoming less common or extinct in some areas? One reason is that the places where ringtails live are gradually disappearing as people build more and more homes and roads in the animals' habitat. Also, as the rivers ringtails live along dry up or become polluted, ringtails are forced to find new places to live and search for food.

Construction (above) and dried-up rivers (right) often force ringtails to find new homes.

Some ringtails have been known to wander onto farms in search of an easy meal. They often kill chickens inside coops. To protect their animals, farmers sometimes kill the ringtails.

In some states, such as Arizona, New Mexico, Colorado, and Texas, **trappers** hunt ringtails for their fur.

Ringtails secrete a foul odor that smells like cat urine if they are cornered or trapped. They do this as a way to defend themselves against predators.

The Future

The good news is that David Wyatt's current research shows that ringtails remain numerous in Sutter Buttes. He still finds it hard to get an exact count, though. "They're **elusive** but also very successful and widespread," said David.

Scientists like David hope that ringtails will continue to thrive. However, this means that the wild places where ringtails **flourish**, such as Sutter Buttes, must be protected. By saving the places ringtails call home, this hidden animal treasure may be saved from an uncertain future.

Though ringtails are losing their homes in many areas, they are able to adapt easily to new habitats.

Ringtail Facts

The ringtails' scientific name, *Bassariscus astutus*, means "clever little fox." Ringtails have a fox-like face and huge eyes that are surrounded by white fur. Here are some more facts about this animal.

Weight	Adult ringtails weigh anywhere from 1.5 to 3 pounds (.6 to 1.4 kg).
Length	24 to 32 inches (61 to 81 cm), including a 12- to 17-inch (30- to 43-cm) tail
Food	Insects, spiders, small animals, fruit, nuts, leaves, and bird and reptile eggs
Predators	Bobcats, coyotes, and great horned owls
Life Span	About seven to nine years in the wild; up to 16 years in zoos
Habitat	Forests, rocky plateaus, deserts, and canyons in the Midwest, the western United States, and Mexico
Population	Unknown

People Helping Ringtails

Habitat loss is the main long-term concern facing ringtails today. There are many people who are passionate about saving ringtails and preserving the habitat they need to live in. Here are two organizations that are hard at work helping ringtails:

Animal Rescue Team (A.R.T.)

- Located in California, the Animal Rescue Team has been helping injured or **orphaned** ringtails and other wildlife for more than 22 years.
- The group also educates the public about wild-animal care and protection and about how to fight animal abuse.
- In 2009, A.R.T. rescued more than 200 wild animals from an area in Santa Barbara, California, that was badly damaged by a fire.

Wildlife Land Trust: The Humane Society of the United States

- The Wildlife Land Trust works to protect wild animals by preserving their natural habitat throughout the United States.
- In 1995, the Wildlife Land Trust set up the Arroyo Alamo Wildlife Sanctuary in Fairview, New Mexico. The 12-acre (5 hectares) sanctuary is home to ringtails, along with many other wild animals.
- Ringtails living in a Wildlife Land Trust area have a better chance of surviving and raising families than ringtails living in heavily populated cities or towns.

Biologists examining a ringtail

Glossary

adapted (uh-DAPT-tid) changed over time

agile (AJ-il) able to move around fast and easily

animal control (AN-uh-muhl kuhn-TROHL) a government group that protects pets and wild animals from dangers that they may find in the wild or when they wander into neighborhoods or towns

biology (bye-OL-uh-jee) the study of animals, plants, or other living things

coatis (koh-AH-teez) animals that have a ringed tail and a long snout and are related to raccoons

crevices (KREV-iss-iz) cracks or splits in rocks

dens (DENZ) hidden places where animals sleep or have their babies

ecologist (ee-KOL-uh-jist) a scientist who studies the relationship between plants, animals, and their environment

elusive (ih-LOO-siv) very hard to catch or find

extinct (ek-STINGKT) when a kind of plant or animal has died out

flexible (FLEK-suh-buhl) able to bend easily

flourish (FLUR-ish) to grow and succeed

habitat (HAB-uh-*tat*) a place in nature where an animal or plant normally lives

litter (LIT-ur) a group of animals that are born to the same mother at the same time

mammals (MAM-uhlz) warm-blooded animals that have a backbone and hair or fur on their skin and drink their mothers' milk as babies

mating season (MATE-ing SEE-zuhn) a time of year when animals come together to have young

nocturnal (nok-TUR-nuhl) active at night

orphaned (OR-fuhnd) left without parents

plateaus (pla-TOHS) areas of high, flat land

preserve (pri-ZURV) a place where animals are kept safe and protected

prey (PRAY) an animal that is hunted by another animal for food

radio collars (RAY-dee-oh KOL-urz) collars that send out radio signals and are put on animals so that their movements can be tracked

reptile (REP-tile) a cold-blooded animal that has dry, scaly skin, a backbone, and lungs for breathing

rotate (ROH-tate) to turn around

solitary (SOL-uh-*tair*-ee) living alone

tag (TAG) to mark an animal in order to identify the animal later on

territory (TER-uh-*tor*-ee) an area of land that is defended by an animal

trappers (TRAP-urz) people who catch wild animals in traps for their fur

vibrissae (vye-BRIS-uh) stiff hairs growing on some animals that help them sense their environment

Bibliography

Bay Nature Institute (baynature.org/articles/jan-mar-2011/where-are-the-ringtails)

Colorado Division of Wildlife (wildlife.state.co.us/WildlifeSpecies/Profiles/Mammals/Pages/Ringtail.aspx)

The Mammals of Texas, Online Edition (www.nsrl.ttu.edu/tmot1/bassastu.htm)

Read More

Gustafson, Sarah. *Little Critters of the Southwest.* Tucson, AZ: Western National Parks Association (1999).

Hoffmeister, Donald F., and Herbert S. Zim. *Mammals.* New York: St. Martin's Press (2001).

Read, Tracy C. *Exploring the World of Raccoons.* Ontario, Canada: Firefly Books (2010).

Learn More Online

To learn more about ringtails, visit
www.bearportpublishing.com/AmericasHiddenAnimalTreasures

Index

Arizona 15, 23

babies 19, 20–21
biologist 6
Burger, Jutta 5

California 4, 15, 16, 23
claws 12, 15
coatis 5
communication 21

dens 7, 19

ears 10
eyes 10–11

feet 14
food 8–9, 10–11, 19, 20
fur 19, 20

habitat 7, 24–25, 27, 28–29
hunting 10–11, 12–13, 15

Irving Ranch Natural Landmarks 5

jumping 12

litter 19

mating 18–19
Mexico 6
Midwest 6
miner's cats 15

nocturnal 10, 12

predators 10, 28
prey 10, 15

raccoons 5, 9
radio collars 17, 22

scent 10
size 8, 19, 28
Sutter Buttes 16, 26

tail 9, 13, 20
teeth 15
territory 18
Texas 25
trappers 25

United States 6

vibrissae 11

Wyatt, David 6–7, 15, 22, 26–27

About the Author

Joyce Markovics is a writer and editor in New York City. She lives with her husband, Adam, and a spirited rabbit named Pearl, who is nocturnal, just like ringtails!